Cherished Teddies™

Giving From the Heart

Special Thoughts of You

Publications International, Ltd.

©1998 Priscilla Hillman.
Licensed by Enesco Corporation, owner
of the CHERISHED TEDDIES trademark.

Quotations on pages 6 (bottom), 11, 27 (top), and 46 written by Priscilla Hillman, artist and creator of the Cherished Teddies™ collection. Other quotations compiled and written by Kelly Womer, a freelance writer whose work has appeared in several national collectibles publications.

Photography by Brian Warling.

Photo styling by Lisa Wright.

Copyright © 1998 Publications International, Ltd. All rights reserved. This book may not be reproduced or quoted in whole or in part by any means whatsoever without written permission from:

Louis Weber, C.E.O.
Publications International, Ltd.
7373 North Cicero Avenue
Lincolnwood, Illinois 60646

Permission is never granted for commercial purposes.

Manufactured in China.

8 7 6 5 4 3 2 1

ISBN: 0-7853-2992-7

GIVING FROM THE HEART

*Charity is doing an act of
kindness not because you're
supposed to but because you know it
will make a difference in the world.*

*The key that unlocks your
heart also opens the door
to caring deeds, gentle words,
and kind thoughts.*

GIVING FROM THE HEART

Giving is not an occasional act of kindness. It's a permanent act of love that has no end.

One can resist temptation, but not a teddie bear.

— Priscilla Hillman

GIVING FROM THE HEART

GIVING FROM THE HEART

A cat purrs. A dog wags its tail. But to know when a teddie bear is feeling happy, just look in his black-button eyes. If they stare back at you (and, of course, they usually do), it will surely be a happy day!

GIVING FROM THE HEART

It's Twice As Nice With You

GIVING FROM THE HEART

GIVING FROM THE HEART

Why do people love teddie bears? Because they don't eat much, never betray a secret, never swear, and never, never steal all the covers.

—Priscilla Hillman

My teddie bear is stuffed with love and happy memories.

—Priscilla Hillman

GIVING FROM THE HEART

To give a part of yourself is to receive the greatest gift of all. It's like finding a priceless treasure in your heart, a special blessing that has been there all along.

Everyone is gifted in some way. Your gift may simply be that you are a good friend.

GIVING FROM THE HEART

GIVING FROM THE HEART

Encouragement walks behind you. Hope walks before you. A friend walks with you.

There is no limit on how far a friendship can take you, as long as you walk together and take each day a step at a time.

GIVING FROM THE HEART

GIVING FROM THE HEART

GIVING FROM THE HEART

*A friend is someone
who will always care
With kindness, joy, and
hugs to share.
A friend is someone who
will always be true.
A friend is someone just like you!*

GIVING FROM THE HEART

Cherish the tender moments ... watching children play in the park, meeting a friend for an afternoon chat, growing a garden in your backyard, learning how to fly a kite, sitting alone by a babbling brook. Embrace them. Share them. Live them.

Giving From The Heart

GIVING FROM THE HEART

GIVING FROM THE HEART

Look inside your treasure chest.
There is a lucky find.
Look inside your heart of hearts.
There is a gift so kind.
Look inside your hopes and dreams.
There is always peace of mind.

GIVING FROM THE HEART

Bear Hug (n.) 1. An embrace given with extra love. 2. Something warm and wonderful, fuzzy and friendly. 3. Something that should never be kept to yourself.

GIVING FROM THE HEART

GIVING FROM THE HEART

When you plant a seed of friendship, you reap a garden of happiness that will bloom forever.

The only things you should keep to yourself are secrets (and perhaps the fact that you still keep a teddie bear close by for special hugs).

Giving From the Heart

GIVING FROM THE HEART

GIVING FROM THE HEART

A teddy bear's real charm is in being huggable.

— Priscilla Hillman

Listen to the voice within, and you'll hear a smile. Listen to your heart, and you'll hear love. Listen to your dreams, and you'll hear your future.

Giving From the Heart

A teddie bear always seems to wear a smile and never seems to wear out of giving love. It's just a simple fact of teddie bear life.

Love is a word that doesn't need to be spoken to be understood. But it needs to be written in your heart to be shared.

GIVING FROM THE HEART

GIVING FROM THE HEART

Make each day a celebration sprinkled with colorful confetti, filled with balloons, and topped with chocolate icing!

Friendship Softens A Bumpy Ride

GIVING FROM THE HEART

Giving From the Heart

Giving From the Heart

The gift of laughter is the gift of life. For in laughing we live, and in living we learn to laugh.

There is more pleasure in loving than in being beloved.

—Thomas Fuller

GIVING FROM THE HEART

Like rainbows after the storms, smiles always follow a frown. Bright and beautiful, they shimmer and shine for all the world to admire.

Giving From the Heart

GIVING FROM THE HEART

GIVING FROM THE HEART

Life is a give and take.
If you have been blessed,
bless others.
If you have been loved, love others.
If you have been encouraged,
encourage others.
If you have been inspired,
inspire others.
If you have received, give.

GIVING FROM THE HEART

GIVING FROM THE HEART

*The best kind of gift is a gift
of kindness, wrapped
in brightly colored paper and tied
with ribbons of love and tender care.*

*When you love someone
all your saved-up
wishes start coming out.*

— Elizabeth Bowen

GIVING FROM THE HEART

You don't have to wait for a holiday or special occasion to give someone a present. There's no better time than the present.

Wake up each morning expecting a miracle. Then you will find unexpected blessings that are sure to come your way.

GIVING FROM THE HEART

GIVING FROM THE HEART

*End each day with an
exclamation point and
begin the next day right
where you left off!*

*Life gives us a new beginning
every day, a new reason
to be thankful, a new chance
to share a good deed.*

Giving From the Heart

GIVING FROM THE HEART

GIVING FROM THE HEART

Don't walk in front of me
I may not follow.
Don't walk behind me
I may not lead.
Just walk beside me
And just be my friend.

—Anonymous

GIVING FROM THE HEART

Prescription for the common cold: rest, plenty of Mom's homemade chicken soup, and one sympathetic teddie bear.

—Priscilla Hillman